SACAGAWEA

Library of Congress Number: 87-4578

Library of Congress Cataloging in Publication Data

Gleiter, Jan, 1947-
  Sacagawea.

  (Raintree stories)
  Summary: Traces the life of the Shoshoni Indian
girl who was stolen from her tribe at the age of
twelve, sold to a French trapper, and served as a
guide in the Lewis and Clark expedition.
    1. Sacagawea, 1786-1884—Juvenile literature.
2. Lewis and Clark Expedition (1804-1806)—Juvenile
literature.   3. Shoshoni Indians—Biography—
Juvenile literature.   [1. Sacagawea, 1786-1884.
2. Lewis and Clark Expedition (1804-1806)
3. Shoshoni Indians—Biography.   4. Indians of
North America—Biography]   I. Thompson, Kathleen.
II. Miyake, Yoshi, ill.   III. Title.
F592.7.S123G55   1987   970.004′97   [B]   [92]   87-4578
ISBN 0-8172-2651-6 (lib. bdg.)
ISBN 0-8172-2655-9 (softcover)

SACAGAWEA

Jan Gleiter and Kathleen Thompson

Illustrated by Yoshi Miyake

Raintree Childrens Books
Milwaukee

It was a hot summer morning in 1805. Two women and a little girl were walking through a valley. They were Shoshone Indians. Suddenly they saw something strange and frightening. It was a group of odd looking men, walking toward them. The men had pale skin. Hair grew on their faces. One woman ran and hid. The other woman and the little girl were so terrified that they could not move.

The strange men came closer and closer. One reached into the pack he carried at his side. The little girl bent her head and closed her eyes in fear. But nothing happened. She opened her eyes. The man was holding out a necklace of beads. It was for her. Then he leaned down and rubbed bright red paint on her cheeks. The little girl knew what that meant. It was a Shoshone sign for peace.

The woman who had run away came back. She, too, got beads. Her cheeks were also painted red by this odd but gentle man. The three Shoshones led the strangers to their camp. On the way, sixty Shoshone warriors rode up on horseback. When they saw the signs of peace and the gifts, they welcomed the explorers.

The leader of the strangers was a man named
Meriwether Lewis. He needed to talk with the
Shoshones. He and his men needed help to go on
with the long journey they were making. But they
could not speak the Shoshone language. And the
Shoshones could not speak their language, English.
But Meriwether Lewis knew that in a few days, the
rest of his men would catch up with his smaller
group. Lewis's partner, William Clark, was leading
the others. With Clark, there was a young woman
who could speak the Shoshone language. Her name
was Sacagawea.

Before Clark and the others arrived, Lewis and the Shoshones could use only sign language. It was not easy to talk this way, and not much could be said. Lewis was able to say that he and his men were friendly. But he could not explain what they were doing in this wild land. He could not explain why their trip was so important.

It is hard, now, to imagine what the United States was like in 1805. Part of it, the eastern half, had farms and towns and cities. But half of it was almost completely unknown. West of the Mississippi River, there were no towns. The few maps that there were showed very little. No one knew what the land was really like, or who lived there.

Oregon Country

Louisiana Territory

Mexico

There were many different Indian tribes across the huge area west of the Mississippi. Each tribe knew the area it lived in and some of the nearby land. But no one had ever crossed the whole unknown territory.

This wild land had just been bought from France, two years before. It was called Louisiana. The Louisiana Territory was much larger than the state of Louisiana is today. It included all of the land between the Mississippi River and the Rocky Mountains.

United Statetes

Florida

Map of North America 1803

At that time, Thomas Jefferson was the president of the United States. President Jefferson wanted to find out what the Louisiana Territory was like. He knew there were rivers. He knew there were mountains. But he didn't know exactly where the rivers went. He didn't know how to get across the mountains. He didn't know what the plants or the animals or the people were like.

Thomas Jefferson sent Meriwether Lewis and William Clark to find out.

Lewis and Clark prepared well for their journey. They bought boats, medicine, tools, flour, and salt. They bought gifts for the Indians they knew they would meet. They bought paper and ink for maps and reports. On May 14, 1804, Lewis and Clark and forty-three other men began their trip from St. Louis, Missouri.

By November, the group of explorers had gone as far as the middle of what is now North Dakota. There they stopped for the winter. The next part of their trip would be very hard. They would have to travel a long way to the Rocky Mountains. President Jefferson wanted them to go all the way to the Pacific Ocean. To do that, they would have to cross the mountains. And they couldn't cross the mountains without horses.

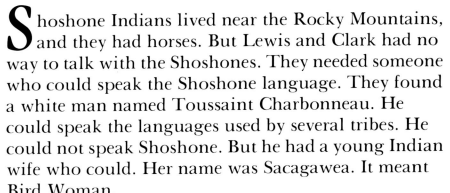

Shoshone Indians lived near the Rocky Mountains, and they had horses. But Lewis and Clark had no way to talk with the Shoshones. They needed someone who could speak the Shoshone language. They found a white man named Toussaint Charbonneau. He could speak the languages used by several tribes. He could not speak Shoshone. But he had a young Indian wife who could. Her name was Sacagawea. It meant Bird Woman.

Neither Meriwether Lewis nor William Clark liked
Charbonneau. He was not a very likeable man.
But they agreed to hire him, if he would bring
Sacagawea along.

When the explorers set out in the spring,
Charbonneau and Sacagawea went, too. A third new
person also joined the group. He was Jean Baptiste
Charbonneau, Sacagawea's baby son.

Although Sacagawea was only about seventeen
years old, she did not behave like a girl. She seemed
older than her years. Perhaps it was because her
childhood had been cut short.

17

Sacagawea could speak the Shoshone language because she was a Shoshone Indian herself. She had been born in what is now Idaho. When she was about eleven, her people had been attacked by a group of Hidatsa Indians. As Sacagawea ran across a river, she was caught and carried away by an enemy warrior on horseback. The young girl was taken far from her family, to live with the Hidatsas. Several years later, Charbonneau won her in a bet with the Hidatsa chief. Sacagawea became his wife.

Now, she was on her way home, back to the land where she had lived with her own people.

By the end of July, the explorers were in what is now western Montana. Sacagawea recognized the land. She told Lewis and Clark that they were not far from her people, the Shoshones.

The group was traveling in boats. Lewis was in a hurry to meet the Shoshones, and the boats were slow. He decided to go ahead on foot with a small group to look for the Indians.

A few days later, Clark was walking behind Sacagawea. Suddenly he saw her begin to dance with joy. She had seen Meriwether Lewis and the Shoshones.

Sacagawea was overjoyed to find several of her childhood friends. One was a young woman who had been captured when Sacagawea was. She had escaped from the Hidatsas and had found her way home. Now the two were together again.

At last the explorers and the Shoshones would be able to talk with each other. They sat in a circle in the shade of some willow trees. They passed a peace pipe. Smoking the pipe was a sign of friendship. The Shoshones took off their moccasins. Lewis and Clark had learned what this meant, so they took their boots off, too. This meant that any promise made would be kept. Whoever broke a promise would walk barefoot forever.

Sacagawea came to sit down with the men. She looked across the circle and saw the chief for the first time since she had arrived. To Lewis and Clark's surprise, she ran to him and threw her arms around him. The chief was her brother!

Sacagawea was able to help the explorers explain
their trip. There was no Shoshone word for
"president." So Sacagawea called Thomas Jefferson
"the Great Father." The Shoshones did not know
what the Pacific Ocean was, at least by that name. So
she said that they wanted to go all the way to the Big
Water.

The Shoshones agreed to sell the horses the
explorers needed. They also promised to send along
several guides to show them the way across the Rocky
Mountains.

When Lewis and Clark left to continue their journey, Sacagawea went with them. Even though her most important job was over, there were many ways she could help.

Sacagawea could point out the best way to go whenever they were passing through land she recognized. She could find roots and berries that were safe and good to eat.

There was another way in which Sacagawea was a great help. Many of the Indians between the Rockies and the Pacific had never seen white people. And they knew that strangers were often dangerous. Without Sacagawea, Lewis and Clark might often have found themselves in trouble. But the sight of Sacagawea and her baby calmed the Indians. They knew that war parties did not bring women and children along. They could tell that the explorers came in peace.

The trip was long and hard. But no matter how bad things got, Sacagawea never gave up. She went all the way to the Pacific Ocean and back again across the Rocky Mountains.

During one part of the journey, Sacagawea walked with her baby on her back for fourteen days. She was wet and cold and hungry almost every step of the way. Today, there is a highway where she walked. Today, people make that same trip in three hours.

The Lewis and Clark Expedition was a great success. Lewis and Clark and their men made it safely back to St. Louis in September of 1806. More had been learned about America's western lands than had ever been known before. Settlers began to travel to this frontier territory. Towns grew where there had been only trees and deer. Railroads were built where there had been only Indian paths.

The expedition might never have succeeded without Sacagawea. For all her valuable help, she got one silver medal. But she got something else, as well. She got a feeling about herself. For all her long life, Sacagawea knew that she had made a difference. She knew that she had done what needed to be done, and done it well.